W9-BCT-277

BOWHUNTING

by Tom Carpenter

Content Consultant
Bill Sherck
Outdoor Television Show Host

SportsZone

An Imprint of Abdo Publishing
abdopublishing.com

Printed in the United States of America, North Mankato, Minnesota
042015
092015

THIS BOOK CONTAINS
RECYCLED MATERIALS

Cover Photos: Bruce MacQueen/Shutterstock Images (background); Martin
Haas/Shutterstock Images (foreground)
Interior Photos: Bruce MacQueen/Shutterstock Images, 1 (background); Martin
Haas/Shutterstock Images, 1 (foreground); iStockphoto, 4–5, 6, 21 (middle), 24,
34–35; Donald Dryer, 9; Ron Chapple/Corbis, 10–11; Paul Tessier/iStockphoto,
13; D. Robert & Lorri Franz/Corbis, 14; Sue Cocking/Miami Herald/TNS/
Newscom, 17; Jeff Vanuga/Corbis/Glow Images, 19; Tom Reichner/Shutterstock
Images, 21 (top); Dennis W. Donohue/Shutterstock Images, 21 (bottom);
Thomas Sbampato/ImageBroker/Newscom, 22–23; Jason Lindsey/Alamy, 29,
40–41; Marcel Jancovic/Shutterstock Images, 30–31; Lee Cohen/Corbis, 32;
Nate Allred/Shutterstock Images, 36; Tim Farrell/The Star-Ledger/Corbis, 38;
Jeffrey B. Banke/Shutterstock Images, 42; Ryan Dorgan/Casper Star-Tribune/
AP Images, 44

Editor: Jon Westmark
Series Designer: Jake Nordby

Library of Congress Control Number: 2015901254

Cataloging-in-Publication Data
Carpenter, Tom.
 Bowhunting / Tom Carpenter.
  p. cm. -- (Hunting)
Includes bibliographical references and index.
ISBN 978-1-62403-832-7
1. Bowhunting--Juvenile literature. 2. Archery--Juvenile literature. I. Title.
799.2/028/5--dc23

                                                    2015901254

CONTENTS

Chapter 1

WELCOME TO BOWHUNTING

It's a cold morning in early November.

Shivering, a young hunter steps into overalls.

She pulls on a roomy jacket, slings her

backpack over her shoulder, and grabs her bow

Ground blinds can conceal movement better than tree stands. This helps the hunter get close to game.

and arrows. She walks down a forest trail and across a field of frosted grass. She arrives near the edge of the woods. She unzips the blind's door, steps in, zips it back up, and gets set.

Does are legal to shoot in many states. But many people prefer to shoot bucks for their antlers.

The landscape slowly comes to life as the sun rises higher. Two bright cardinals dart through the brush. A raccoon shuffles past.

Suddenly a white-tailed doe appears. The deer walks 20 yards (18 m) away, heading for the woods. It stops, flicks its tail, and looks back.

The young archer begins to draw her bow. Any deer is a trophy, especially when taken with archery gear. But then the hunter hears something else. A buck is coming too! It is mating season. The buck is following the doe.

The hunter draws her bow, settling into her anchor point. She has practiced this shot many times. The buck pauses only 15 yards (14 m) away.

Thwack! The arrow finds it mark. The buck leaps into the air, kicking its hind legs. It scampers off. The bowhunter listens. She hears a crash in the woods, followed by some thrashing in the leaves. Fewer than 50 yards (46 m) into the woods, the young hunter spots the downed deer. As she approaches it from behind, she sees that it is dead.

The young bowhunter kneels next to the large six-point buck. She smiles with the pride of harvesting a wild animal with a bow and arrow.

Bowhunting through History

Bowhunting has been around for thousands of years. It was part of the Native-American way of life in North America. Native Americans hunted with bows made of wood and backed with animal tendons to make them springy. Hunters crafted arrows from wood and arrowheads from flint or other stones.

In the early 1900s, most hunters used firearms instead of bows and arrows. Game populations decreased because of overhunting and habitat loss. Many hunters wanted to limit how many animals were killed. One way to do this was to make hunting more challenging by using archery gear instead of firearms. Bowhunting as a sport became more popular in the 1950s. Famous archer Fred Bear filmed hunts for others to watch. He also started

Legendary bowhunter Fred Bear, *right*, poses with a prize bear in Ontario, Canada, in 1943.

a company that made bows and other archery gear for hunters.

Bowhunting is now more popular than ever. Like all forms of hunting, bowhunting takes special techniques, equipment, and shooting skills. But hunters enjoy the challenge.

Chapter 2

TECHNIQUES

Hunting with archery gear can be more difficult than hunting with a firearm. A bow limits the distance a hunter can shoot. A hunter can kill a white-tailed deer, mule deer, or elk at 200 yards

Most bowhunters do not use scopes. They rely instead on open sights.

(183 m) or more with a rifle. A bowhunter can shoot from a top distance of approximately 30 yards (27 m).

The bowhunter must know the quarry and put good hunting techniques to work to get close to the animal. Bowhunters often pursue deer, elk, pronghorns, bear, small game, and game birds.

Scouting

Successful hunters often scout before they hunt. They walk the land they plan to hunt, looking for game trails and signs of animals, such as droppings and tracks.

Next they "glass" the hunting grounds. This means they go quietly to a high point and use binoculars to look for game. It is best to do this at dawn or in the evening, when animals tend to move around.

Hunters can also go online and study satellite photographs of the hunting area. They can zoom in and look at fields, brushy areas, waterways, and forests. This helps them understand how the game might travel.

Game cameras are important scouting tools too. These cameras strap to trees, poles, or fence posts and take pictures and video of animals that pass by. This lets hunters know when and where game animals roam

Game cameras give hunters important information about where and when animals pass by.

the land. Once a hunter knows how animals are using an area, it is time to hunt.

Tree Stand Hunting

White-tailed deer are a popular bowhunting target. One great way to hunt whitetails is from a tree stand. A tree

Hunting from a tree stand helps a hunter stay out of the deer's line of sight and avoid detection.

stand is usually 12 to 18 feet (4–5 m) off the ground. It gets the hunter above whitetails, where they do not expect danger. It also offers a better view for the hunter and may keep some of the hunter's scent above whitetails' sensitive noses. Tree stands also help bowhunters hunt mule deer and elk.

It is important to scout to find the best place to put up a tree stand. One good spot is along a deer trail between feeding and bedding areas. This is best in the late afternoon and evening, when deer are moving from their daytime hideouts toward nighttime feeding areas.

Hunters must position their stands with wind direction in mind. The wind should blow from the deer to the hunter. Otherwise whitetails will smell the hunter and never come close. If the wind is wrong for a particular tree stand, hunters should avoid that stand.

Ground Blind Hunting

Sometimes scouting reveals a good spot for game, but there are no trees suitable for a tree stand. Other times

Tree Stand Preparation

Hunters trim branches and brush around their stands to create a couple of narrow but clear shooting lanes. They also cut lanes approaching their stands so they can walk quietly to them. It is a good idea to set multiple stands for different wind conditions. If the wind is wrong for one stand, it may be right for another.

the habitat has few trees or none at all. A portable blind is good for these situations.

Portable blinds are easy to set up. They blend in well against brush, cattails, and tall grass, or in a corner between fences. Hunters set up downwind of where the game is expected. Hunting from a ground blind works well for white-tailed deer, mule deer, and pronghorns.

A hunter in a ground blind is not invisible from game, though. It is smart to close the back window and lower the side windows so deer cannot see through. Hunters should also minimize movement and noise. Wearing a camouflage face mask and gloves may help hunters go unnoticed. Successful hunters often practice shooting out of a ground blind before the hunting season begins.

Spot-and-Stalk Hunting

Sometimes game is spread out in mountains or wide-open prairies. This is good for spot-and-stalk hunting. People

Ground blinds often have adjustable windows that allow hunters to control the direction they hunt.

frequently hunt mule deer, pronghorns, and open-country whitetails in this way.

The first step in spot-and-stalk hunting is spotting. Bowhunters move along high points of hills and ridges. But they do not walk along the top. Otherwise animals will see their outline against the sky. They move into the wind and look carefully for game. Sometimes hunters stop at high

Water Hole Pronghorns

One of the best ways to hunt pronghorns is from a ground blind at a water hole. Pronghorns need to drink every day. Hunters can scout to find the pond or water hole pronghorns use. Then they set up a blind downwind, climb in before sunrise, and wait. Pronghorns might come to the water at any time to drink. The animal may fake a drink several times, jerking its head up to look around. When the pronghorn starts drinking, the hunter can pull up the bow, take aim, and shoot.

points. They use binoculars or spotting scopes to look for game.

The second step is stalking. Good hunters take time to plan how they will approach the animal. They use terrain and vegetation to hide their movement and work to keep the wind in their favor.

Bugling Up an Elk

One exciting bowhunt involves pursuing elk during their mating, or rutting, season. The hunter starts by going into elk habitat before dawn and listening for males, called bulls, bugling. Bugling is a whistling call elk use to attract females, called cows, to breed. The call also challenges

Spotting scopes are more powerful than binoculars. They help hunters get close-up views.

other bulls to fight. Often a bull will come looking for the source of the bugling.

Cow calls can also attract bulls. It is best to hunt with a partner when calling for elk. One hunter sets up 50 yards (46 m) ahead of the calling hunter. This is because the approaching elk often get suspicious and stop short of the call.

Tracking after the Shot

One of the most important skills in bowhunting is being able to follow an animal's blood trail after the shot.

Few big-game animals drop on the spot when hit by an arrow. The arrow's broadhead is designed to slice arteries, veins, and organs. This causes the animal to lose blood and die. But the animal usually runs before going down.

Hunters should pay close attention to where animals are located when they shoot them. This helps hunters find their targets' blood trails. Hunters should wait at least half an hour before attempting to follow a blood trail. If a hunter follows too soon, the animal may keep running.

It is good to trail the animal in pairs. One person follows the blood trail. The other looks for the animal and is ready to shoot. A well-placed arrow is lethal. Most deer will fall within 100 yards (91 m) of where they are shot.

SHOT PLACEMENT

Broadside: This is a good shot, especially for larger animals. The arrow has a good chance of hitting the vital organs and killing the animal.

Quartering Away: This is the best shot for bowhunters. The arrow has a good chance of avoiding the rib cage and killing the animal.

Quartering Toward: Animals approaching at an angle or head-on are not good to shoot with a bow. The arrow is likely to hit a bone and fail to kill the animal.

Chapter 3

EQUIPMENT

Bowhunting requires smart scouting and good attention to detail for success. But a bowhunter also needs to equip properly for the hunt.

Bows

Bowhunters use one of four types of bows.

Longbows are the most basic bow. Their range

is limited to approximately 20 yards (18 m).

Longbows are traditional and are usually built

23

The shape of recurve bows adds extra speed to arrows leaving the bow.

from wood. Native Americans built and used longbows before European settlers came to North America.

Recurve bows have limbs that curve back toward the front of the bow. Recurves shoot arrows faster and farther than longbows, with a reliable range of approximately

25 yards (23 m). Most recurves are made of laminated wood or fiberglass.

Compound bows use a system of wheels, cables, and pulleys to launch arrows faster and with more power than recurves and longbows. The wheels on a compound bow allow the archer to hold 50 to 80 percent less weight when the bow is pulled back. This allows the hunter to hold the bow on target longer. A compound bow is accurate and effective to around 35 yards (32 m). Highly skilled archers can place arrows consistently at slightly farther distances.

Crossbows are becoming more popular for hunting deer. A crossbow consists of a small but powerful bow mounted on a stock similar to a rifle's. The hunter draws the bow back by hand or by mechanical crank until it locks into place. When the hunter pulls the trigger, the bolt releases. The bolt is a short arrow. Crossbows can be very accurate because they require less muscle power to hold on target. They shoot more like a firearm.

Legend:
- Legal during archery deer season
- Legal only during firearm season
- Legal only for physically challenged hunters
- Illegal

Only four states allowed crossbow hunting during archery seasons in 2000. Today it is legal in 28 states.

Crossbows are accurate up to 40 yards (37 m). Many states and provinces are beginning to allow hunters to use crossbows.

Arrows

Every bow needs arrows to shoot. Longbow and recurve hunters often use traditional wooden arrows.

Most compound bows use arrows made of aluminum or carbon. Aluminum arrows are heavier and wider than carbon arrows. This makes them fly more slowly. Carbon arrows fly fast and flat toward the target. But carbon arrows tend to cost more.

Crossbow bolts are made of carbon and carbon composites.

Flu-Flu Arrows

A Flu-Flu is a special arrow with extra large fletching. The arrow flies straight and fast for 25 to 30 yards (23–27 m). But then the large fletching slows the arrow down. Flu-Flus are perfect for bowhunting small game like rabbits or squirrels. The arrows do not fly far. This makes them easier to find. There is less of a chance of the arrows skipping under leaves or into tall grass.

Heads and Broadheads

Bowhunters need a variety of heads for their arrows. Aluminum and carbon arrows often have inserts that allow hunters to screw in different heads. Bowhunters usually switch heads for practicing and hunting. But they can use the same arrows.

Bowhunters practice shooting with field points and blunt tips. Field points are pointed and made for shooting at targets. Blunt tips are flat. They are better for shooting at stumps or dirt piles.

Broadheads are best for hunting. Broadheads have sharp, cutting blades. It is important to sight in a bow with the broadheads that will be used for hunting. The point of impact for a broadhead may be different from that of a field point or blunt tip.

Most modern broadheads have removable blades that can be replaced if they become dull. There are also broadheads with blades that can be sharpened. Some broadheads have retractable blades that stay folded in as the arrow flies. The blades pop open only when they hit the target.

Hunters using compound bows use a trigger to release the bowstring.

Releases

Once a bow is at full draw, the string has to be released. Most recurve and longbow shooters use a shooting glove or finger tab to hold the string and protect their fingers from the moving string. Hunters with compound bows use a release aid that holds the string until a trigger on the aid is pulled. Crossbow shooters pull a trigger on the stock that is like a rifle trigger.

MAKING THE SHOT

Release Aid:
A release aid distributes the weight around the hunter's hand and allows for a smooth release.

Fletching or Vanes: Feather fletching or plastic vanes stabilize the arrow in flight.

Pulley: Pulleys help hunters draw the bowstring back on compound bows.

Quiver: A quiver holds extra arrows and keeps the tips enclosed.

Silencer: Silencers go on the bowstring to keep it from vibrating loudly when released. Noise could cause the animal to move.

Since most bows do not have scopes, binoculars are important for spot-and-stalk hunters.

Bowhunters need good optics. Binoculars are essential for seeing game at long distances when spot-and-stalk hunting. Binoculars also help in forest, brush, and other close-range situations where the hunter needs to pick game out as it walks through or hides in cover.

Most hunters use 7- or 9-power, full-size binoculars. Compact binoculars do not gather light well at dawn or dusk. This can make it hard to see.

Range finders tell the hunter how far away a target is. Hunters cannot have range finders out all the time. So many people identify distances to fixed objects. This way when an animal appears, they know how far away it is.

Camouflage Clothes

Bowhunters usually wear soft, camouflaged clothing. This helps them stay quiet when moving.

Camouflage clothing sometimes comes with scent-blocking technology. If clothing does not have scent blockers built in, many hunters use a spray bottle or wash-in mix that reduces scent. But even with scent blockers, hunters need to know how to use the wind to their advantage.

Chapter 4

SHOOTING A BOW

The processes for shooting a longbow, recurve bow, and compound bow are very similar. But most hunters practice with a single bow to become consistent.

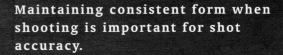

Maintaining consistent form when shooting is important for shot accuracy.

Stand

The bowhunter stands perpendicular (at a 90-degree angle) to the target. This offers the archer more power to draw the bow and hold it on target.

Some shooters use the corner of their mouths as anchor points.

Grip

The shooter grips the bow solidly but without squeezing. Squeezing too hard twists the bow, making it so the arrow does not fly straight.

Extend

The bowhunter extends the bow out and locks the elbow into place.

Draw

Next the hunter pulls the bowstring back. If using a release aid, the mechanism is engaged onto the string before the draw. The shooter should not use a bow that is too hard to draw back.

Anchor

Consistent shooting requires the same anchor point after each draw. The shooter's hand or release aid must sit at the exact same place each time. Some hunters tuck their thumb into the bottom corner of their jawbone for consistency.

Aim

The bowhunter puts the proper sight pin, dot, or crosshair on the target and holds steady. The shooter breathes easily and exhales.

Practice shooting helps hunters be calm and confident when they get a shot at an animal.

Release

The release must be smooth and consistent. With a release aid, the trigger squeeze is steady and gentle. Good archers do not jerk, or the arrow will fly off course. Some bows do not have a release aid. In this case, good archers simply relax their fingers to release their arrows. They do not open their fingers.

Follow-Through

Good shooting form requires distinct follow-through. The best archers keep holding the bow up loosely until the arrow hits the target. They do not drop the bow and look to see where the arrow goes.

Watch

It is important to watch the arrow closely. Bowhunters should remember where the animal was when they hit it. This allows them to go right to the spot when it is time to look for a blood trail. To prepare for hunting, hunters watch the arrow fly all the way to the target.

Overcoming Buck Fever

"Buck fever" is when an animal comes close enough for a shot and the hunter gets extremely excited, nervous, or shaky. Some adrenaline is fine. But buck fever can make hunters unable to shoot. The best way to beat buck fever is to practice archery consistently. Breathing slowly and deeply can also help a hunter calm down when the moment comes.

Practice

Many bowhunters practice their archery skills year-round. They shoot regularly to stay in top form. Then when a shot at game comes, they are accurate and automatic.

Chapter 5

SAFETY AND CONSERVATION

Bowhunting may seem safer than hunting with a gun, but there are still several important safety considerations. It is also important to understand bowhunting's place in wildlife conservation.

Tree Stand Safety

Bowhunting is often done out of a tree stand. But tree stands can be dangerous. It takes a

Arrows can become exposed if handled improperly.
Following safe practices helps avoid injury.

special set of safety rules to put them up properly, climb
into them, and stay safe while in them.

Safe bowhunters erect and secure their tree stands
according to manufacturer instructions. They also use
safety straps when putting up stands and climbing
into them.

It is dangerous to climb with a backpack or other equipment. Many hunters pull up their equipment using a rope.

To be safe, hunters should always use safety straps when climbing into and out of their stands. It is also important for hunters to climb down if they get too tired to hunt. If they fall asleep, they may fall from their stands.

Once in place, it is smart to check stands every year to be sure the bolts and straps are still good and the tree is healthy. Nailed-up or homebuilt tree stands are not reliable. They could result in serious injury from a fall.

Broadhead Safety

The razor-sharp blades on broadheads can be extremely dangerous. Falling while holding a broadhead can cause bad cuts. Most bowhunters use quivers with hard-shell covers that hide the broadheads. It is not safe to walk with an arrow on the bow. Tree stand or ground blind hunters should put away arrows before moving about.

Bowhunting allows people of many ages to enjoy the outdoors while mastering a new skill.

Conservation

Conservation is the smart use of natural resources. Bowhunting is a form of conservation. Bowhunting any type of animal is challenging. This means that bowhunters get to spend a lot of time outdoors without impacting animal populations much.

But good hunters are often successful. It is important that hunters use as much of their animals as possible. Game must be field-dressed immediately. This cools the meat and prevents it from going bad. Many hunters know how to butcher meat so that it is all utilized and savored. But local butchers will often process deer too.

Bowhunting is a good hunting method in today's world. In many places, humans have intruded on game habitat. There is not enough room to hunt safely with guns. But many towns, townships, and counties allow bowhunting. This is a great way to hunt close to home.

No matter where you hunt, it is always essential to obtain the proper licenses and tags. Hunters must also follow all relevant hunting regulations. This includes dates, limits, and tagging procedures. Putting a tag on an animal shows the authorities that it was harvested legally. Most tags are also cut, notched, or signed when used so they cannot be used again.

GLOSSARY

anchor point
The place to which an archer draws the bowstring back.

blind
A portable, tent-like structure used to hide from game.

broadhead
A triangular arrowhead with sharp edges.

draw
To pull the bowstring back.

fletching
Feathers on an arrow, which stabilize it during flight.

glass
To look for game using binoculars or a spotting scope.

optics
Devices that help hunters zoom in to spot, watch, and study game.

pronghorn
An animal similar to an antelope that is common on the western plains of North America.

quarry
The game a hunter pursues.

quiver
A holder that carries an archer's or bowhunter's arrows.

shaft
The long, main part of an arrow.

FOR MORE INFORMATION

Further Reading

Frazel, Ellen. *Bow Hunting*. Minneapolis: Bellwether Media, Inc., 2013.

Graubart, Norman D. *How to Track a Deer*. New York: Windmill Books, 2015.

Llanas, Sheila Griffin. *White-Tailed Deer*. Minneapolis: Abdo Publishing, 2014.

Websites

To learn more about Hunting, visit **booklinks.abdopublishing.com**. These links are routinely monitored and updated to provide the most current information available.

INDEX

ABOUT THE AUTHOR

Tom Carpenter is a father, a sportsman, and an outdoor writer. He has introduced many children, including his three sons, to the thrills and rewards of hunting. A native son of Wisconsin who always has part of his heart in South Dakota, he planted roots in the middle. He lives with his family near the shores of Bass Lake, Minnesota.

11-15